Johann Sebastian Bach

The Three Violin Concerti

in Full Score

From the Bach-Gesellschaft Edition

Dover Publications, Inc.
New York

Published in Canada by General Publishing Company, Ltd., 30 Lesmill Road, Don Mills, Toronto, Ontario.
Published in the United Kingdom by Constable and Company, Ltd.

This Dover edition, first published in 1986, contains the three violin concerti (BWV 1041 in A Minor and BWV 1042 in E Major, both for solo violin and accompaniment; and BWV 1043 in D Minor, for two solo violins and accompaniment) from Vol. 21 (the 4th vol. of *Kammermusik*) of *Johann Sebastian Bach's Werke*, edited by Wilhelm Rust and published by the Bach-Gesellschaft, Leipzig, in 1874 (intended for 1871).

Manufactured in the United States of America
Dover Publications, Inc., 31 East 2nd Street, Mineola, N.Y. 11501

Library of Congress Cataloging in Publication Data

Bach, Johann Sebastian, 1685-1750.
  [Concertos. Selections]
  The three violin concerti in full score.

  Reprint. Originally published: Leipzig, 1874 (Johann Sebastian Bach's Werke ; v. 21)
  Contents: For violin and orchestra in A minor, BWV 1041—For violin and orchestra in E major, BWV 1042—For two violins and orchestra in D minor, BWV 1043.
  1. Concertos (Violin with string orchestra)—Scores. 2. Concertos (Violins (2) with string orchestra)—Scores. I. Bach, Johann Sebastian, 1685-1750. Concertos, violin, string orchestra, BWV 1041, A minor. 1986. II. Bach, Johann Sebastian, 1685-1750. Concertos, violin, string orchestra, BWV 1042, E major. 1986. III. Bach, Johann Sebastian, 1685-1750. Concertos, violin, string orchestra, BWV 1043, D Minor. 1986.
  M1112.B33   1986   86-750557
  ISBN 0-486-25124-1

Contents

(All three concerti were composed in Cöthen between 1717 and 1723. The orchestra for all three consists of Violins I & II, Violas and Continuo.)

Concerto in A Minor, BWV 1041

6   Concerto in A Minor

Andante.

8   Concerto in A Minor

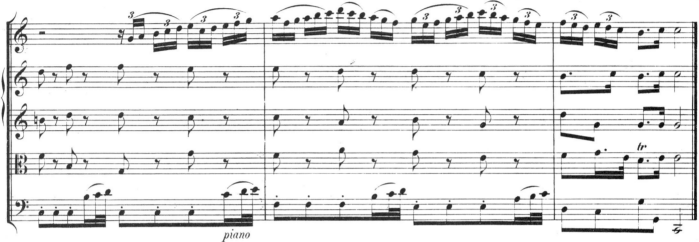

Allegro assai.

Concerto in E Major, BWV 1042

18   Concerto in E Major

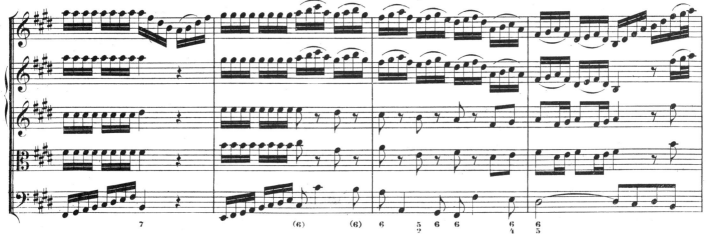

Concerto in E Major   21

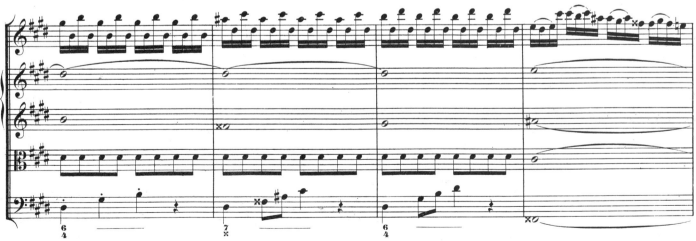

Adagio.

Allegro.

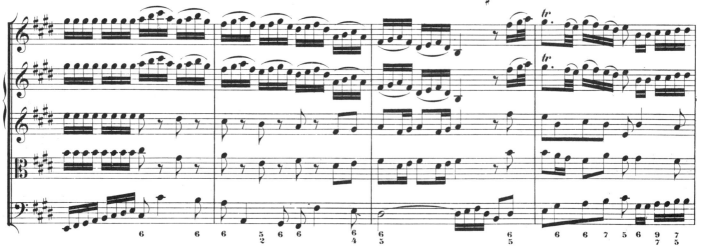

Concerto in E Major 25

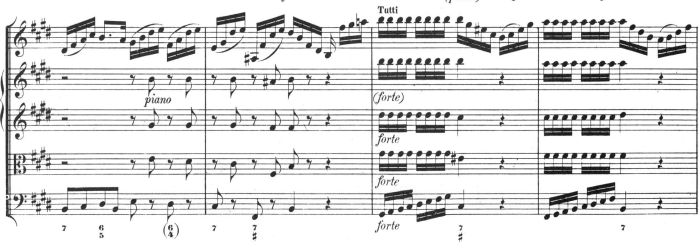

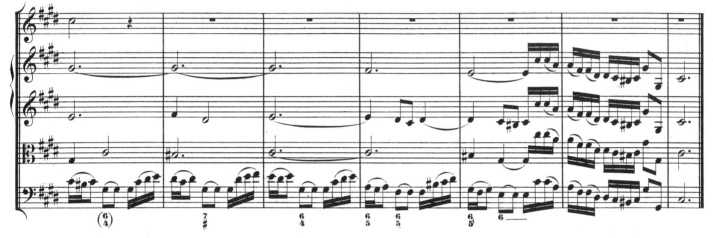

Allegro assai.

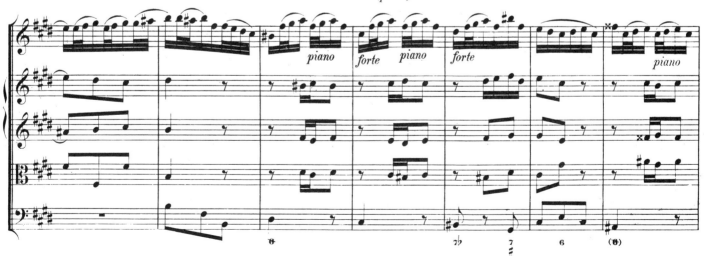

Concerto in D Minor, BWV 1043

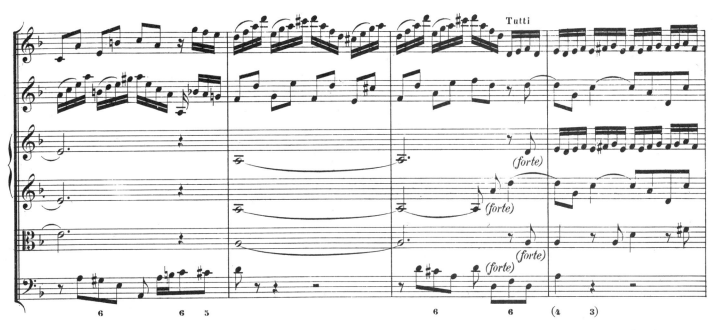

Largo ma non tanto.

44 Concerto in D Minor for Two Violins

Allegro.

Concerto in D Minor for Two Violins

Concerto in D Minor for Two Violins   47

48   Concerto in D Minor for Two Violins

Concerto in D Minor for Two Violins   49

50   Concerto in D Minor for Two Violins